MW01141702

"Beth Barany's 7 _____
that will prove esp _____
for fiction author _____
site to advance their writing careers."

—Joel Friedlander,
WWW.THEBOOKDESIGNER.COM

"*Twitter for Authors* presents easy to digest tips and strategies that any author can use, even those who are shy or hate social media. The book is especially helpful for fiction authors with specific examples of ways to connect with potential readers of your book. In fact, one of the tips was so brilliant that revealing it here would be a spoiler. If you've been mystified by how to use Twitter powerfully to build your author platform, this is the book for you!"

—Lynne Klippel,
Publisher and Best-Selling Author of
Overcomers, Inc., BUSINESSBUILDINGBOOKS.COM

"If ever there was a bluebird of happiness for meaningful tweeting, it's Beth Barany. When you read *Twitter for Authors*, have your note-taking pencil ready."

—Carolyn Howard-Johnson,
Author of the multi award-winning *The Frugal Book Promoter*, BUDURL.COM/FRUGALBKPROMO

"*Twitter for Authors: Social Media Book Marketing Strategies for Shy Writers* is filled with ideas to get you tweeting up a storm in no time flat! In an age when platform defines the success of a book, put these strategies into action immediately and watch your writing career grow."

—Cheryl Patrice Derricotte,
Author of *Being The Grown-Up: Taking Care of Someone with a Terminal Illness*

"*Twitter for Authors* delivers the best reasons for tweeting I've yet to read. Barany is not only instructive in the *how*, she also explains the *why* behind a social media segment that looks like a stormy sea of undifferentiated opinions. With a copy of *Twitter for Authors* as your life raft, you'll be ready to jump in!"

—**Catharine Bramkamp**,
Producer of the Newbie Writers Podcast,
Author, Blogger, & Newbie Tweeter

"There's nothing more tragic to me than a brilliant writer with a distinct voice—and no audience. *Twitter for Authors* will help you find your tribe, build your platform, and boost your book sales."

—**Mark Malatesta**,
Founder of *Literary Agent Undercover,* and former
New York Times Bestselling Literary Agent

"Beth Barany has done a phenomenal job with this book; I highly recommend it for anyone looking to improve their online brand or simply connect with others in Twitter Land."

—**Vangile Makwakwa**,
Author of *Heart, Mind & Money: Using Emotional
Intelligence with Money*

"You're an author ... maybe you're a previously traditionally published mid-list author ... or an emerging indie author. If you are just now coming to the realization that YOU are your marketing machine, you have come to the right book choice in Beth Barany's clever little guide. *Twitter for Authors* is chock-full of savvy advice, and links (some old, some new)—but all that give a perspective on where Twitter has been and where it's going. Be a Smart Cookie, grab Beth's guide and start 2013 right, you'll have SUCH a much better understanding of the value of Tweeps, Twitters, and Tweeting!"

—**Emily Hill**,
Author of the *Ghost Chaser's series*

"In *Twitter for Authors* you will find everything you need about using social media successfully. By reading this book, you will get more exposure and sell more books. This book will tweet you right."

—**Brian Jud**,
Author of *How to Make Real Money Selling Books*

"I believe that Twitter is essential for authors and this quick guide will help remove some of that fear you may have about embracing this powerful social network. If you're looking for an easy primer for getting started, this is it!"

—**Stephanie Chandler**,
Author of *The Nonfiction Book Marketing Plan* and
Founder of NONFICTIONAUTHORSASSOCIATION.COM

"If you think that social media and online marketing are only for techies, kids, and super-geniuses, Beth is here to help. *Twitter For Authors* holds your hand and walks you gently through the start-up phase, reassuring you each step of the way. All that's missing is milk and cookies and it would be just like going to grandma's house to hear stories about how to expand your platform as an author and sell more books!"

—**Bryan Franklin**,
Global Top 1% Business Coach for Entrepreneurs

"Beth Barany's *Twitter for Authors* presents very engaging, intriguing methods of using Twitter to build buzz for a new book, enliven interest in back list books, and even generate buzz for a book yet to be written. The door is wide open for the strengths of social media such as Twitter to 'generate curiosity, start the conversation' and to make connections. The benefits of using Twitter are clearly laid out. Barany herself has over 11,000 people on Twitter following her. For a shy and non-tech author like me, Barany's book makes the lure of connecting with my audience through social media, which I have fumbled about with for some time, irresistible."

—**Carolina Montague**,
Author of *Door in the Sky* and *Sacred Guardian*

"As an author and as a huge fan of Twitter, I applaud Beth Barany for her book, *Twitter for Authors*, that provides easy-to-follow steps—and encouragement—to help authors dip their toes into the waters of social media relationship building. For all you authors afraid of the water, you can safely come in now with Beth's book as your guide."

—Phyllis Zimbler Miller,
Author of *Top Tips for How to Market Your Book on Amazon and Facebook*

"Reading only a few paragraphs into the Introduction to *Twitter for Authors* was enough to change my approach to this most wicked and enchanting mode of communication for writers. As a Twitter-baby, I was led along with a gentle and encouraging hand by Beth Barany's enthusiasm and superb understanding of this particular social medium. *Twitter for Authors* is a book I will keep and refer to often as a guide to marketing and social media etiquette. This is a must-read for anyone planning to join the tweeting fray and avoid all the social media *faux pas*."

—Leigh Verrill-Rhys,
Author of *Wait a Lonely Lifetime*

"Beth Barany's *Twitter for Authors* is the perfect guide for outlining your social media game plan. The activity sections at the end of each chapter are particularly helpful in motivating you to build your own social media blueprint and the real life examples in the book help put the tips into a context that seems achievable for authors of all types."

—Molly King,
BOOKBABY.COM—Self Publishing Made Easy

"The vast majority of people on Twitter are just wasting time. Their Twitter activity is not generating significant new sales for their business. In this one-of-a-kind book, Barany provides tactical guidance specifically for fiction authors, designed to expand their reach and further their careers. This is a 'must read' for fiction writers navigating the often confusing world of social media."

—Patrick Schwerdtfeger,
Author of *Marketing Shortcuts
for the Self-Employed*

"If you're the shy, retiring type of author who breaks out in hives at the mere mention of 'marketing' and 'social media,' Beth Barany's *Twitter for Authors* is for you. Replete with good, simple, concise information and step-by-step guides and practice activities, it shows you how (signing up, posting) and why (to connect with people with similar interests, build an audience, and potentially increase sales of your book) to use Twitter. Barany demystifies the social media phenomenon by breaking it down to its barest essentials: an instant messaging service on which you can write three sentences sharing with other Twitterers what you had for dinner, the dog you just adopted, the great wave you just caught at Maverick, and how you love the book you just finished reading. The followers you create by connecting with other, like-minded people may just lead to them checking out your book and even buying it when it comes out. Barany herself has more than 11,000 Twitter followers so she knows whereof she speaks. Do everything she says!"

—Mandy Behbehani,
Author, *The Blasphemy Box*

"I've been an Author Success Coach for almost ten years and this is what I've learned. Writers are like fearful woodland creatures. The hardest thing to convince them to do is take the leap into the social media unknown. Beth Barany has taken twitter by the scruff and shaken it into submission, presenting techniques for everything from writing a strong profile to promoting an event. This is a simple, practical blueprint to help authors see the brilliant power of the twitterverse!"

—Deborah Riley-Magnus,
Author of *Finding Author Success*

"In *Twitter for Authors: Social Media Book Marketing Strategies for Shy Writers,* Beth Barany has created a valuable resource for writers new to Twitter as well as experienced Twitter users. Short, succinct chapters fit easily into a writer's busy schedule. The activities at the end of each chapter help the reader apply the knowledge to his or her own life. Readers will come away with a better understanding of what their goals are for using Twitter and how best to achieve those goals in a time efficient manner. All while having fun!"

—Vanessa Kier,
Author of bestselling The Surgical Strike Unit series

Twitter for Authors

Social Media Book Marketing
Strategies for Shy Writers

by Beth Barany

Barany Publishing
Oakland, CA

We publish books that empower authors
to have successful careers.

Barany Publishing
771 Kingston Ave. Suite 108
Piedmont, CA 94611
WWW.BARANYPUBLISHING.COM

Contact Beth:

Email: beth@bethbarany.com
Website: WWW.BETHBARANY.COM
Blog: WWW.WRITERSFUNZONE.COM/BLOG
Twitter: TWITTER.COM/BETH_BARANY
Facebook: WWW.FACEBOOK.COM/BETHBOOKCOACH

Legal Disclaimer

Although the author and publisher has made every effort to ensure that this writing guide is complete and accurate, we take no responsibility for individual state laws. This writing guide is for informational purposes only and readers with questions should consult the appropriate legal and accounting authorities.

This book is solely the author's opinion and does not guarantee any results from reading it, though results can be obtained. All results from reading this book belong to the reader.

All resources listed in this writing guide are to be used at the reader's own risk. Links are included to point you in the right direction, but you should do a thorough investigation of any vendor that you choose to use.

Web links were correct at the time of printing. As the web changes constantly, some links may not be accurate at a later date. Please do let me (Beth Barany) know if you find any broken links. Email me at beth@bethbarany.com.

Dedication

To all the shy writers out there who want their work to be
read and appreciated.

Table of Contents

WHY YOU SHOULD READ THIS BOOK

You're a fiction writer, a novelist. Perhaps you're starting your first novel and want to know what this Twitter and social media thing is all about. Perhaps you've been writing for a while and are getting ready to send your manuscript to agents and editors and know you need some kind of social media presence. You may be wondering if Twitter is right for you. Or perhaps you've been using Twitter for socializing and now want to use it to build a presence with your potential readers, fans, and supporters. If you find yourself in one of these groups, then this book was written for you.

Wherever you may be in your fiction writing adventure, this book is also for authors who would like to become comfortable using Twitter, as well as other social media tools, to market their books and their message, so that you can share your stories with the world.

I'm assuming that you'd like more readers, you'd like to sell more books, and you'd like to have time to do what's most important to you: write more books.

Additionally, this book is for shy introverted fiction and creative nonfiction book authors, who want tips and tricks on what works best, and are willing to experiment with different things to find what works for you individually.

This book is also for authors who are ready to take charge of their publishing careers through social media book marketing. Whether you're independently published, self-published, with a small press, or published by a big publisher, great! You came to the right place. I believe in helping authors learn what they need to know so they can take charge of their careers.

By the time you're done reading this book, my goal is to help you feel more comfortable with sharing your books on Twitter, on other social media channels, and even in person. I'll help you feel clear about how to use Twitter, help you feel satisfied from the experience, and help you create connections between you, your fans and supporters.

While I wrote this book primarily for fiction writers, nonfiction writers will find these tips useful, too.

Adapted from blog posts and articles, I wrote this book in bite-sized pieces for quick and easy consumption in this busy world. This book will help you get inspired, take action, smile, and share what is meaningful and useful. Read this book in order, or bounce around to what you need.

INTRODUCTION

Just so we're clear up front, this isn't expressly a how-to book, though you will get some step-by-step instructions. For those of you who need the how-to aspects of social media, the process changes so frequently that what works today may not work tomorrow. So I decided it best to leave the how-to information to YouTube and up-to-date online articles to teach the how-to aspects. I focus on the best ways to use Twitter as a fiction writer with a short overview of social media, and I'll even include the what, why and some of the how of Twitter. To that end, I'll help you create a game plan for using Twitter, and other social media channels. Lastly, I'll end with how independent authors have been using Twitter and other social media tools. At the end of each chapter, I'll share a short activity to help you focus and take the next step.

I'm first and foremost a fiction writer. I'm also an introvert. I'd rather be in my own little world than focusing on marketing my books and my message. But the hard truth about being in business for yourself—and that is what it really means to be a published writer—is that you need to let people know about what you do and make it easy for them to say, "Yes! I like it!" And then you need to make it easy for them to buy your books.

INTRODUCTION

I practice what I preach. Before I learned the tools and strategies I share in this book, I was afraid of putting myself out there. Ever since I started playing around with Twitter, Facebook and LinkedIn in 2009, I've been diving into social media and trying new things all the time. Sometimes what I do works. That is, it gets me the results I want. Sometimes my actions don't. But I don't know which things work until I try, as I hope you will.

Some of the results I've received from using Twitter and other social media tools include new clients, new fans and supporters, book reviews, interview opportunities, and book sales.

To show you what you can accomplish, here are some specifics results I've had as of this writing: I have 11,364 people on Twitter following me and I am following 7,536 people; I have 5,275 Facebook friends and 398 subscribers; 1,033 Facebook Fans on my three fan pages; and 1,150 newsletter subscribers.

What this book isn't covering: I'm not covering Facebook in any depth. That may be a topic for a future book.

Also what this book is not: This book isn't saying that Twitter is the be-all and end-all of your marketing and social media efforts. People are always looking for the quick fix. Twitter isn't it. No one tool is a quick fix. Yet how you use it makes the difference between succeeding and ho-hum-ing it. Get clear on your value to your readers. I'll be covering how to do that in this book.

Though I'm not here to convince you about the benefits of social media, I do recommend you consider how social media can help your author career: Social media is great for generating curiosity about your offerings, your message, and your products (and/or services); it's a great way to have a conversation with fans, supporters and colleagues you wouldn't otherwise meet. Facebook, Twitter, LinkedIn, and other networks are great vehicles for letting people know about your expertise: your ability to create an awesome experience through your novels. These networks aren't for direct sales or even direct marketing, but are for letting people get to know you and the experience you create through your novels.

In my opinion, social media is all about making connections between human beings and building relationships. As you go forward in this book, remember:

- Social media is a great way to generate curiosity and start the conversation, which is the first stage of sales. A two-way street.
- Marketing is really just a way to share your message with people your message who don't already know you. It is a one-way street.

- People pass along your message if you give them something meaningful to share. Touch their hearts or punch them in the gut, metaphorically speaking, and people will share your book with their friends.

Now go ahead and discover this wonderful world of social media. Remember, no one's forcing you down a straight and narrow path. You can either start with Chapter 1, or find a chapter in the table of contents that appeals to you and start there. Enjoy!

Chapter 1: A Pep Talk, or Increase Your Book Sales Before You Write Your Book

Is it possible to increase your book sales before you write your book?

Anything is possible, and I now know that you can do a lot to increase your chances before you ever write a word. As writers, we know that a good book is the best way to get readers interested in what we write next.

The real question is: Are you willing to take the risk to market your book well?

As an introvert it is risky to look outward to the readers and ask the readers: What do you want?

My first impulse when I considered book marketing was to run away.

I wanted to run from looking outward at my potential readers because I'd rather daydream about my novel than figure out how to market my own books.

Similarly, most novelists prefer to look inward and experience their story world rather than look outward and talk to real people. I've felt that way for years.

Also, I've felt screwed. Pardon my language. I mean, the books I've published—what about them? I can't go back in my handy-dandy time machine to market and sell those books before they're written.

Chapter 1

I do know the number one thing I can do to increase my sales is to let my audience know about me, my books, and most importantly, how my books can benefit them. I can market and sell my books years after they have been published.

Easier said than done, right?

Yes, and I'm doing it—marketing and selling my books—and so can you.

This book is about marketing and selling your books, specifically with Twitter, by being active online with the intent to serve, with activities to increase your contacts, readers, and connections.

One way I've figured it out is to get in there, try stuff, do stuff, play. I will help you do the same. This book aims to help you take concrete, small, and do-able steps so that Twitter will be a part of your book marketing efforts.

The tips shared in this book do work. That said, do what you really enjoy doing. Sometimes you may not know what that is. In that case, I recommend you experiment with different activities in this book. That's your job: to determine what you really enjoy! What may work for one person may not work for another. I'll do my job: Guide you through stepping out into the world of Twitter with the intent to help you sell more books and build your author career.

Activity Guide

☐ Take stock of where you'd like to be in relationship to Twitter. For example, maybe you'd like to be following and connecting with book reviewers. Maybe you'd like to be finding fellow authors to get emotional support as you work on your writing.

☐ Then, notice where you currently are. Maybe you have close friends and family on Twitter. Maybe you don't have an account, yet.

That's it for now. You can relax.

Chapter 2: Using Twitter to Network and Market Your Books

In addition to a website, a newsletter, and a blog, authors can use social networking tools to connect with friends, make new friends, interact with current readers, and gain new readers. In this chapter, I explore the wonders of Twitter, and how you can use it now to share with the world about your book.

What is Twitter?

In their own words, Twitter is "a real-time short messaging service that works over multiple networks and devices."

By short message, they really do mean short. Messages are only up to 140 characters long, including spaces and punctuation. That's approximately one to three sentences. Another way to think of Twitter is that it is a microblog. People use it to write about anything and everything, from what they ate for lunch, to reporting breaking news as it happens, to promoting some cool service or product they found or are offering.

I share examples of what writers tweet in Chapters 10 and 11.

Why Use Twitter?

I use Twitter because it's fun! It's a great way to procrastinate. Yes, it's both of those things, and I think it does what social networking does best: It connects us with others of like mind.

In just 140 characters, you can tell your followers about your latest book, a cool tip, or what you ate for breakfast—if that's what is important to your audience. It's a way to foster a new fan base, and reach out to people already active on the Internet. Chances are they'll surf over to your site and see what your book is about. As a lot of Internet marketers say, "Traffic is King." (Conversion, or getting people to take action, is Queen.)

Let's pause a moment and define these important terms: traffic and conversion. Traffic is defined as how many people are coming to your site. Conversion is how many of those visitors take the action you'd like them to take: i.e., sign up for your newsletter, subscribe to your blog, buy your book, follow you on Twitter or connect with you on one of the other social media networks.

Another way of looking at it is "website traffic multiplied by conversion equals results."

Website Traffic x Conversion = Results

Thanks to MARKETINGTERMS.COM for this equation.

Award-winning paranormal and historical romance author Carolyn Jewel (TWITTER.COM/CJEWEL) likes Twitter a lot and says, "You don't need any skills besides some basic literacy and you don't have to spend hours updating and creating content, adding information, or feeling bad that you haven't done those things or checked the site." (WWW.CAROLYNJEWEL.COM/)

How to Set Up Your Twitter Profile

Setting up your profile on Twitter requires less time than Facebook because it only asks for a user name, a website, and a bio in 160 characters or less. Therein lies the power of Twitter. Forced to communicate in short segments, you get to write something interesting and useful at the same time. Like Facebook, you can also invite and connect your email lists. People "follow" you in Twitter. You have "followers." You are "following" others.

How to Use Twitter

Depending on what you want to reveal, your posts could be either a micro back-cover blurb teaser, semi-personal posts about your daily life, a tweet about a cool resource you found online, or talking up another author's book. For those of you who already maintain a blog or site, Twitter is also a great way to send people to your blog. Always add a URL to send people to your book, blog, or site. Use BITLY.COM to shorten your long web address to twenty-five characters, thus saving space for content. Twitter will also shorten website links for you, but using BITLY.COM allows you to track how many times people click on your URL.

How to Build Followers on Twitter

This is the question people ask me the most. The answer is simple, but not easy. (There are always decisions to make!) Find others to follow and others will in turn follow you. Some of them will, anyway. After you've invited people from your email accounts, find people with common interests, by location, or with keywords by using Twitter's Advanced search tool:

SEARCH.TWITTER.COM/ADVANCED (You can use this feature even if you're not logged in to Twitter.)

Search using keywords like book reviewer, historical romance (or whatever your genre is), author, or literary agent, etc. You can also search for like-minded people by searching for interests such as favorite movies, TV shows, bands, books, etc.

I follow people I think would be interested in what I have to offer. They can choose to follow me or not. You can opt to approve those who ask to follow you, or you can let anybody follow you. I find it's best to let anybody follow you. You never know who a potential reader may be. I am selective, however, about who I follow. I only want interesting and fun people, usually writers, and other creative types, book industry professionals, and also leading-edge tech people.

For Jewel, Twitter is "exponentially more effective and important than the 'traditional' [social networking] sites."

I agree. The people you follow become a community, and create a conversation that flows around the world. With Twitter you can be a part of that conversation, one you might not normally be a part of.

Note: When I find someone interesting to follow, I check out their followers, and if I like them, I follow those folks too.

In addition to the ability to connect with potential readers, you can connect with bookstores, libraries, agents, editors, reviewers, columnists, publishers, and experts in the book publishing and marketing world. Here are two to get your started: the London Book Fair (@LondonBookFair) and the *New York Review of Books* (@nybooks).

Jewel adds, "You suddenly have a community view that you would never have if you didn't happen to be an insider yourself. Your view of that community is suddenly bigger, richer, more intimate, and far more informed. You simply cannot get that from MySpace, Facebook or your blog. And, within that community, your voice is heard, too. You're in the conversation and some portion of it is, in fact, all about you. On purpose. Your followers want that."

So, come join the conversation, and have fun in the process. Twitter takes only a little bit of time and can broaden your reach as an author.

Resources

To learn more about Twitter, I recommend you check out the *New York Times* article, Sept. 7, 2008: "How Twitter can help at work" (SHIFTINGCAREERS.BLOGS.NYTIMES.COM/2008/09/07/HOW-TWITTER-CAN-HELP-AT-WORK/) Though this *New York Times* article was written a few years ago, its point are still relevant today.

Dani at Blog Book Tours has a nice bit on how to use Twitter for your book promotion, and great stuff on how to promote your book via a blog tour! Check out her link here: WWW.SQUIDOO.COM/QUICKEST-BLOGBOOKTOURGUIDE-EVER.

Check out the Twitter Help pages, if getting started in Twitter tweaks you out. But really it's quite easy! In case you'd like more support, go to Twitter's support link: SUPPORT.TWITTER.COM/.

And for fun, and to see how I use Twitter, Follow me! At TWITTER.COM/BETH_BARANY.

Activity Guide

☐ Open your account on Twitter and find at least one person you know. That could be me or one of your writing buddies.

☐ Follow at least one person.

Chapter 3: Playing a Social Networking Game You Can Win: An Introduction

As a writer, you may think that social networking is waste of time. And you're right. It is—if you don't create a game plan, and play a game you can win.

Before we get into why, let's define social networking. Now also called social media. (It's one of my favorite topics, ever.) According to Jace Shoemaker-Galloway, a feature writer on SUITE101.COM, social networking "refers to a community where one connects and communicates with others on the Internet," including blogs, instant messaging, email, video, chat rooms or forums, Twitter, Facebook, Pinterest and LinkedIn.

For published authors, social networking is a way to share our books with new audiences, increase sales, and connect with supporters. For as-yet-unpublished writers, social networking is a way to find an audience, find allies, and build our lists.

An ally is a person who supports you on this precarious and wild journey as an author: authors in your genre, book reviewers, agents, editors, industry pundits, librarians, fans, and anyone who thinks what you're doing is cool. For authors at any stage of their career, social networking is about community, connection, and sharing.

NOTE: There are no rules that say you NEED

to be involved in every social networking platform. That said, it's in your best interest to be where your readers are. Take some time to research that. Popular with many readers are sites like GoodReads, Shelfari, and LibraryThing, and the behemoth, Facebook.

Play a game you can win. Games are play. Coming to social networking as a game can create a lightness and joy that can be conveyed in the way you communicate online, and help you create genuine connections. In Chapter 15 I'll explore in more detail how to play a winning game.

Activity Guide

☐ What does winning with social media mean to you?

Chapter 4: Your Clear Message: Get Your Potential Readers Curious Now

Many authors think that book promotions are about giving away swag (or tchotchkes, if you prefer)—like bookmarks, key rings, coffee mugs, etc.—to get attention for their books. But actually, book promotions start with one of the most powerful yet overlooked methods of promoting your books: by what you actually say.

Word of mouth still sells more books than any other promotional tool out there.

Aspiring authors: You can use this tool now, too. Yes, promotions for your author career can begin now, even before your book is published or even completed.

If you state what you write in a way that generates curiosity, you can get more people engaged with what you write, and ultimately they can become your avid fans and book buyers. Bonus: All on a zero budget!

What if you could share what you write in one sentence and immediately know if your listener was curious or not about what you write?

Once a potential reader is curious, then you can ask for her email for your newsletter list (you have one, right? If not, check out MAILCHIMP.COM for an easy and free way to get started with your newsletter.), or if appropriate, invite her to your online home of choice (blog, website, Facebook page, etc.).

So, how do you generate curiosity?

You learn to talk about your story in a compelling and interesting way. You create a Clear Message.

There are four ingredients to constructing this concise, one-sentence description of your book. The goal of this exercise is for you to design a statement that easily rolls off your tongue, and answers the questions we get at meetings, conferences, parties and even in the grocery store checkout line: "What do you write?"

Once you've created your Clear Message, you can adapt it for use in your bio or profile that you create for Twitter, Facebook, your site and your book. (See Chapter 5 on how to write your Twitter profile.)

In this chapter I will help you nail down the four ingredients you need to create your Clear Message:

1. Your genre
2. Your audience
3. Your audience's desired result or experience: what they want
4. Your intended action upon your readers

#1:Your Genre

What is your genre? Stating that you write

"romance" or "fantasy" may be good enough for some of your readers. For others, you may want to be more specific, like "paranormal romance," "epic fantasy," "historical romance," etc.

For example, I say, "I write young adult fantasy novels."

When choosing how to state your genre, think about where your readers would find your book in a brick and mortar or online bookstore. Ultimately, imagine about how your readers categorize what you write. Or ask them!

Action Step: I recommend you browse the bookstores and libraries to pinpoint exactly where your book would fit.

Q: How do you create a Clear Message if you write more than one genre?

A: In today's world of writing multiple genres, I recommend you create a Clear Message for each genre in which you write.

#2: Your Audience and What They Want

In my workshops when I present this part of the Clear Message to romance authors, they often struggle with it.

It's just women, right? They ask.

Well, yes. Now let's get more specific, because we know that not every novel appeals to every person.

Ask yourself: What kind of readers does your work appeal to the most?

Action Step: Describe your audience by specifying what they desire when they read the type of book you write.

For example, your readership could be "women who want an out-of-this-world adventure," "middle-age Midwesterners looking for a sweet escape," or "savvy women needing to break free from their busy lives."

What readers want when they read fiction is an experience.

It's your job as the author to pinpoint and describe that experience as powerfully and succinctly as possible.

Remember: The goal of this exercise is to be able to easily state out loud your Clear Message.

Q: To help put yourself in the shoes of an avid reader, what do you experience when you read your favorite novel?

A: I get the experience of a delicious escape and a thrilling ride. (That's my answer. What's yours?)

#3: Your Intended Action Upon Your Readers

Once you know your genre, your audience and

what they want, look at your intended action upon your readers.

When I get to this part in the workshops I teach, I often get quizzical looks, so I'll start with an example of how I answer the question: "What do you write?"

"I write young adult fantasy to empower teen girls to be the heroes of their own lives."

My intended action upon my readers is to empower them. In fact, this desire to empower my readers permeates all of my writing—fiction and nonfiction, and all my work with writers. (Fancy that! In fact, this verb you choose may be the core of the impact you desire to have in the world.)

What do you want to do for your readers? Some intended actions could be:
- Inspire
- Motivate
- Transport
- Challenge
- Help
- Guide
- Other?! The possibilities are only limited by your imagination!

In my workshops on Social Media for Authors, here are some Clear Messages my authors devised:

"I write romantic suspense novels that invite women to experience the heart pounding rush of danger, action and romance."

"I write middle grade stories that develop kids' self-acceptance and self-assurance through their love of horses and country life."

"I write suspense novels that thrill adults interested in Jewish themes to challenge their personal relationship with Judaism."

"I write historical and contemporary romances to awaken the soul and ignite the imagination of women of all ages to realize their own potential."

"I write erotic urban fantasy for savvy men and women to experience more vitality in their lives."

"I write sensual paranormal romance that inspires women to feel rapture and the power of true love."

And for nonfiction:

"I write how-to guides for fiction authors to help them have successful careers."

"I write inspired stress relief books that help attorneys and other overwhelmed professionals thrive purposefully 24-7."

"I write about the history behind the mythology of original sin to inspire truth seekers."

"My audio tutorials guide fantasy writers to draw on the wisdom of their extra-conscious resources to develop compelling, character-driven stories."

Are you curious about any of these? Notice what grabs you and what doesn't. Okay, authors, your turn!

Action Step: Put all four ingredients of the Clear Message together into one sentence, and say it a few times so it becomes natural, a part of you.

Then practice, practice, practice with friends, family, and colleagues. Revise as needed. Then practice some more. Next, spring it on acquaintances and strangers. Notice how people respond. Are they curious? Great!

When people express curiosity, ask them for permission to add them to your promotion lists. Or, if more appropriate, invite them to connect with you online. If they're not curious, you can ask why.

They may say that they're not interested in the genre you write. In that case, you can get curious about what they do like to read and chat about that. People love talking about their favorite books and movies. If they say that they didn't get what you were saying, you can revise it with them, getting more specific, or making your Clear Message shorter.

What's Next for Your Clear Message

Post your Clear Message as part of your online bio on Twitter and Facebook, as part of your bio when you're a guest blogger, and use it in your signature line of your email.

One of my workshop attendees, author Sharon Hamilton (WWW.SHARONHAMILTONAUTHOR.COM) shared with me a unique way she uses her Clear Message. (From the list above, Sharon's Clear Message is: I write sensual paranormal romance that inspires women to feel rapture and the power of true love.) She said that her Clear Message has a honing beacon to guide where she wants to go with her writing. "[My Clear Message] is the standard," she added. "The personality of my writing."

You too can use your Clear Message to guide your writing as you write and to generate curiosity in your community and beyond.

We're all waiting for your stories. Spread the word!

Activity Guide

☐ Craft your Clear Message.

☐ Share it with your writer friends.

Chapter 5: How to Write Your Twitter Profile

This chapter focuses on how to use your Twitter bio to show off your author platform to its best advantage.

Many authors think their Twitter profiles or bios are a place to put everything but the kitchen sink, and that will make them interesting to readers. Or they do the opposite and make themselves mysterious and only understandable to people who already know and love them.

We're on Twitter to gain a following, to get people curious about what we offer, and to have some fun. Right?!

So make your bio work for you! A smartly written bio can attract all the right readers like bees to honey. An ineffective bio is a missed opportunity, a cry for help, and denial that social networking can ultimately help you build your platform and yes! help you sell more books. Assuming that is what you want.

Your Twitter Profile

Aside from your picture and what you say in your tweets the only other real estate on Twitter for grokking*who you are is your profile.

Chapter 5

Your Twitter Profile: What is it?

Your Twitter profile can only be up to 160 characters long (characters, spaces, and punctuation included). You edit it under Settings/Profile. You put your website in its own field. Once you complete your profile, you can change it whenever you like.

In fact when I learn new things or get an inspiration, I adjust my Twitter profile, tweaking it according to how I want to highlight myself based on what I just learned.

Your Twitter Profile: What do I write?

I'm going to answer the question of what to write in your Twitter profile with a series of questions that will help you elicit all the useful information you'll need to compose this short biography.

- How do you want to be thought of by your readers?
- What is the one important thing you want readers to know about you?
- What can you say that displays your personality and gives a flavor of your writing?

Yes! We're writers and we can show all those things in our Twitter profile.

Look at what these authors have done in their profile. As my coaches say, learn from the best, and surround yourself with winners!

For location, you can put whatever you want. In

my first example, Zoe Winters writes, "undisclosed bad man's lair" for her location.

Note: When you set up your account on Twitter, you'll be asked to choose a public name. This name, often called a handle, follows the @ symbol. As to what to use as your Twitter handle, I recommend you use your name. After all, that is what you sell your books under, right?

Zoe Winters: @zoewinters
Lover of all things fang-related. Subscribe to my newsletter and get KEPT free. Send a
blank email to: freekept@gmail.com

Shelley Munro: @ShelleyMunro
A New Zealand author who writes steamy stories for Ellora's Cave, Samhain Publishing, Carina Press and Liquid Silver Books. When not writing she loves to travel

Renee Pawlish: @ReneePawlish
Master wordsmith, hiker, cyclist. Creator of #IAHB - Indie Author Handbook. Read Nephilim Genesis of Evil, the Reed Ferguson mystery series, and more.

Karen Woodward: @woodwardkaren
I share writing and publishing links. I'm a writer, avid blogger and coffee lover, perhaps not in that order. All my heroines have a bit of Buffy in them.

Chapter 5

Notice that some of these authors state the title of their latest book. But what do you do if you have a forthcoming book that doesn't even have a title, or maybe you're not ready to release the title? Still let us know that you're coming out with a book, or what your hobbies are to generate curiosity. (Curiosity is the first stage in the sales process.)

Your Twitter Profile: Put it All Together

Think of a haiku or a telegraph. Short. Powerful. Use punctuation for emphasis. Periods or hashtags. (I explain hashtags in Chapter 9.) Write several versions. Use the one that pushes the edge, or makes you laugh. Or shocks you.

Here's my Twitter profile in August 2012:

Beth Barany: @Beth_Barany
Award-winning YA epic fantasy author: Henrietta The Dragon Slayer. As Publishing Coach & Consultant, I empower authors to have successful careers! #DrWho geek

Go for it! Draft your Twitter profile. If you'd like me to take a look at it just mention me on Twitter by using @Beth_Barany and ask me in a tweet to give you feedback and support. I'd be happy to! We're all in this together!

Activity Guide

☐ Draft your Twitter profile.

☐ Post it and ask for feedback from a friend.

---

*"Grokking" is from the Oxford English Dictionary. "To grok" means 1. to understand (something) intuitively or by empathy; 2. to empathize or communicate sympathetically; establish a rapport. From: Stranger in a Strange Land by Robert Heinlein, 1961.

Chapter 6: Promotions on $0 Budget: Use Twitter for a Purpose

Twitter is a lot of fun—I'd be the first to admit it. And it's a time suck. In researching this chapter I spent WAY too much time playing on Twitter, doing good things—which I'll get to later—but it's distracting nonetheless.

My plan: Set a time to write the chapter (done!) and a time limit on Twitter. (I'm going to have to work on that one!)

You may think that using Twitter is a complete waste of time. Really, though, Twitter is a goldmine of promotional opportunities for authors. If you use Twitter to grow your fan base, build your book buzz, and ultimately sell your books, then Twitter can be worth all your time away from your current work in progress. Yah!

Overview of the Twitter Basics

To get started on Twitter, here's a review of the steps:

1. Create a free account and fill out your profile information.

2. Choose a picture, background, and bio that stays aligned with your brand. (If you don't know your brand yet, then go with who you are as a writer. You can always change these details as you make decisions about your brand.)

3. Import your contacts from your email account.

4. Then start searching for your favorite authors, media folks, and interesting people to follow.

About Following

In Twitter, the people you follow won't necessarily follow you back, though they may. You also don't have to follow those who follow you. I do recommend you follow your fans, once you've identified them. Which leads us to our first main opportunity: Grow your fan base.

How to Address a Tweet to Someone

Whether you're a newly published author or have a few books under your belt, Twitter is a great way to have direct and timely contact with your readers. By direct, I mean you can send them a message via Twitter called a direct message or DM for short.

Regarding DMs, individuals can only send you a direct message if you're following them. So, follow back if you want to use this feature.

You can also write a Twitter post or a tweet directly back to someone and mention them. Mention a person by their Twitter name with the @ in front. So, my Twitter name or handle is @beth_barany (TWITTER.COM/BETH_BARANY).

Author Ann Aguirre's Twitter handle is

@MsAnnAguirre (Twitter.com/MsAnnAguirre).
Everyone likes some Twitter love.

Actual Twitter Example: @ann_aguirre We'll miss you while you're gone. Enjoy DRAGON AGE

Every one of your followers can see this tweet, and Ann will likely be notified by email that I mentioned her. All of her followers will see this tweet, too.

For as-yet-unpublished authors, you can use Twitter too! Connect with your potential fan base by chatting (DMing in Twitter parlance) with fans of your favorite authors. Share about your favorite authors of the genre in which you write. When it comes time for you to chat about your first book, they can get excited about your book and become your fans.

Continue the conversation by occasionally inviting followers to visit your site or blog and to sign up for your newsletter, if you have one, or to sign up for your RSS feed for your blog.

Build Your Book Buzz

You can build buzz around your book by getting other people to share your news for you. One way to do this is to talk about other people's books a lot, as do Ann Aguirre, paranormal romance author, Twitter.com/MsAnnAguirre, and romance author, Bella Andre, TWITTER.COM/BELLAANDRE, among many others.

Another way to build excitement is to interact with some key influencers: book reviewers. By following romance author, Carolyn Jewel's Twitter (@cjewel; TWITTER.COM/CJEWEL), I found LimeCello (@limecello; TWITTER.COM/LIMECELLO), an avid book reviewer who interacts with the authors she reviews and raves over. It was fun to follow her posts about various authors and see them answer back.

Find book reviewers by using Lists, a new Twitter feature that allows you to collect groups of Twitter folks under one list. Anyone can create a list. I'm sure I was not the only one to create one for book reviewers: TWITTER.COM/BETH_BARANY /BOOK-REVIEWERS. Check out the reviewers' sites to be sure they cover your genre, and then engage the right ones in a Twitter conversation.

While it may be difficult to track book sales because of Twitter, you can increase your author platform—the size of your audience—by using Twitter to point out how great and awesome you are! I mean, how your books rock the house. Or, how absolutely smart and snarky you are. Whatever fits your book, your style, and your author brand.

Links mentioned in this chapter:

List of book reviewers on Twitter:
TWITTER.COM/BETH_BARANY/BOOK-
REVIEWERS

Book reviewer, LimeCello:
TWITTER.COM/LIMECELLO

Romance author, Bella Andre:
TWITTER.COM/BELLAANDRE

Romance Author, Carolyn Jewel:
TWITTER.COM/CJEWEL

Paranormal romance author, Ann Aguirre:
TWITTER.COM/MSANNAGUIRRE

Activity guide

☐ Follow your favorite writers on Twitter or find new authors to follow.

Chapter 7: When Writers Tweet: 5 Hot Tips for Finding and Keeping Your Twitter Groove

By Guest Author, Caroline Jaffe-Pickett

If you had told me that I would ever have been "named" a writer to follow on Twitter, or had an excerpt from my fiction reprinted on a leading blog, or gained over 1,000 followers fairly quickly, I would have tweeted a rather inarticulate, "huh?" leaving me 134 characters left for further self-denial and shock.

I confess, I was one of those Twitter early non-adapters. It wasn't so much that I didn't like Twitter, but like many others I had met, I really didn't see the point. Every time I tweeted, I felt like no one cared, and vice-versa. What did I care what other people had eaten for breakfast? I had like 10 followers, for the longest time—something of a blow to my writing ego. I had, after all, published fiction, nonfiction, and poetry. I had won contests, and read out loud, at respectable places like libraries and schools, and for up to an hour—a lot longer than 140 characters' worth. How long does it take to recite one tweet?

My first few months of tweeting were pretty pathetic. I tried to be clever, and didn't even impress myself. I tried quotes from famous authors, and realized that was so not original. I had read about being authentic, but if I had to try to be authentic, wasn't that—well—disingenuous?

I tried joining in on other Twitter conversations, and was somewhat ignored—the kiss of death in social media. The real life analogy isn't so great either. It's like people walking away from you at a party. Not good. I tried Tweetdeck and it crashed my system. I wanted to try Seismic Desktop, but given my previous "crash," the name intimidated me. Tweetlater changed to "Social Oomph," and I just couldn't handle that. Who named anything "Oomph?"

And what was "Follow Friday," anyway? Was I supposed to find someone I liked and follow them around town? What if they saw me? And forget hashtags. Hash was either something you sautéed in a pan with eggs when you were feeling brazen, or else referred to a period of life one just didn't talk about.

Fortunately, changed happened, and not a moment too soon, as I was going nowhere fast in Twitterland. I attribute the changes (yes, they were good) to some best practices I picked up along the way. That's where my tips come in. I developed them over time, but I know they will help you pick up speed and relevance using Twitter.

1. Observe.

First, I started observing more, and learning about what others in the Twittersphere were retweeting or re-blogging in my topic area: social media, communications trends, writers, books, fiction, and the like. I started to get a feel for what was trending, and what content lent itself to being retweeted and shared.

2. Strategize.

I knew that engagement was key, so I devoted several weeks focusing on strategy and carefully choosing those I wanted to follow, and I developed criteria for both following and finding followers. And what about my blog? Maybe connecting the feed to Twitter would be good. I learned cool tips, like not merely tweeting the title of the blog post, but asking an interesting question, or creating some "teaser" copy to get people interested in clicking onto the Twitter link.

I was growing a pretty good following on Facebook, so I decided to link my Twitter and Facebook temporarily (they are now unlinked—it's better to have distinct content for each of your social media profiles) and that gave me a jumpstart in growing my community. I had started making videos and really enjoyed that, so why not tweet the YouTube links?

3. Embrace Interactivity.

I learned the importance of interactivity and growing an online community, so I made it a point to answer every direct message or question I received on Twitter. I also changed my Twitter style, by avoiding simple updates and sprinkling in my added take on things when I tweeted, based on my opinions and experience, so it was clear I wasn't just "on automatic."

4. Free your "Monkey Mind."

I learned to "free my monkey mind"—the random thoughts I had when driving on the highway or waiting in line at Safeway. The "mini-marketing" lessons going on in my head crying out to be shared were suddenly viable and publishable. I learned that it was OK to loosen up a little in Twitterland.

5. Appreciate Mobile and Use Your Apps!

Once I got an iPad, my Twitter world changed, mainly as a result of Twittelator, one of my favorite apps that allows me to easily tweet actual photos (not just the links) from my media library, and offers a range of icons and even a music feature to tweet song links. It's important to find your favorite and most relevant apps, and stick with them. I had been using Hootsuite as a social media manager, for example, but found I really enjoyed the simplicity of Buffer for updating multiple accounts, including Twitter. (Editor's note: Buffer refers to BufferApp.com/.)

With regular use of Tips #1 through 5 (rinse, repeat, you get the idea ...) cool things started to happen. Fellow writer Sharon Hurley Hall named me one of 39 writers to follow. Other social media "influencers" who I had highly respected, were suddenly following me. "They like me ... they really like me!" I thought to myself, admittedly feeling just a tad more validated. Not that I needed that or anything.

At one point, I was writing a creative piece inspired by the "Balloon Boy" incident that had hit the national news in October of 2009. (Think Colorado and strange silver balloon floating across TV screens for hours, remember?) The incident struck me as a metaphor for modern life, but that's an existential tweet, or story, for another time. As an experiment, I tweeted my story in excerpts for about 10 days. It so happened that I was going to be traveling, and wanted to keep my tweets a-comin'.

Elizabeth Searle, a great fiction writer, (author of Tonya & Nancy: the Rock Opera) and former classmate from Oberlin College, discovered it, liked it, and reposted it on her "Celebrities in Disgrace" blog, which features in-depth and an incredibly humorous analysis of how the mighty can fall. Her blog is based on her novella, which was released as an award-winning film. So ... great experiment, right?!

I had been struggling with a topic for my first e-book, but ironically, Twitter (of all things!) saved me. I combined my best Twitter blog posts with experiences such as the "Balloon Boy" reprint, and voilà.

So, in summary, here are my 5 hot tips for finding and keeping your Twitter groove:

1. Observe   2. Strategize
3. Embrace Interactivity
4. Free Your Monkey Mind
5. Appreciate Mobile and Use Your Apps

About The Guest Author

Caroline Jaffe-Pickett (carrie@carriefreelance.com) is an award-winning writer, editor, and communications specialist, focusing on blogs, e-newsletters, and social media. In addition to consulting, she works as a senior marketing manager for a large San Francisco Bay Area nonprofit.

Please join her at WWW.CARRIEWRITERBLOG.COM, her website, WWW.CARRIEFREELANCE.COM, on Facebook at FACEBOOK.COM/CARRIECOMMUNICATIONS or on Twitter, of course, TWITTER.COM/CARRIEWRITER. Her free e-book, "6 Degrees of Twitteration," is available at: SCRIBD.COM/DOC/103738816/TWITTERATION.

Chapter 8: Chat on Twitter: The What and How of Author Chats on Twitter

This chapter focuses on one of my favorite aspects of Twitter: author chats, both on the informal and the formal ones. These chats allow us writers to go from focusing inward on our current work-in-progress, to focusing outward and networking with other authors and industry professionals. We become better writers and sales people of our products—our books—when we network, IMHO. (IMHO is the acronym for In My Humble Opinion.)

Informally, authors can participate in an ongoing discussion by using a hashtag and a phrase. Some of my favorite ones are self-explanatory, once you see them.
- #amwriting
- #amediting
- #writing
- #writegoal

For more author and writing related hashtags, check out my list on my book's website: WWW.TWITTER-FOR-AUTHORS.COM.

When I dive into the day's editing or writing, I often use these hashtags to tell other writers what I'm up to, and then I sometimes offer and receive support. It's nice to know that we're all in this together! I especially love chatting with my friends Down Under. Because of course I'm writing at night and they're up in the afternoon having their day.

Formally, chats take place at regular times, sometimes sponsored by other writers, sometimes by industry professionals. Here are a few: (I've participated in the first two.)

• #askagent
• #yalitchat
• #litchat
• #journchat

More Twitter chats are listed here: INKYGIRL.COM/WEEKVIEW/.

All within the comfort of my own home, these chats allow me to connect with other writers and get advice from professionals. I love networking this way! Sweet!

To participate in these chats, you can use TWEETCHAT.COM or participate directly on Twitter by searching for the specific conversation with its corresponding hashtag.

From participating in live chats or just by using a hashtag, you can connect with other like-minded people, learn something new, and share about your book.

Activity Guide

☐ Search one of the author hashtags on Twitter by using the search bar on TWITTER.COM.

☐ Then tweet in reply to other's posts.

☐ Post a few tweets using your hashtag of choice.

Chapter 9: How to Use Hashtags on Twitter to Connect with Your Readers

This chapter is focused on something I learned from Kristen Lamb's book, *We Are Not Alone: The Writer's Guide to Social Media*. (She's going to think I'm a stalker! I can't say enough nice and gushing things about her book!) There it is on page number ... Oh I can't remember. You'll just have to read it for yourself. Anyway, she talks about thinking like your reader. By that I mean think about all the other things they like in addition to the type of book you write.

If you write young adult fantasy and your books are sparked by fairy tales, informed by hero stories, and feature a strong heroine, chances are you'll attract readers who like Xena, Bones (the TV show), La Femme Nikita (movies and TV shows), all kinds of fairy tales, and other young adult fantasy tales set in fantasy worlds, like Kate Constable's books, Sharon Shinn's tales, and the Golden Dawn series.

So what does all of this have to do with Twitter?! Glad you asked.

A lot of authors only blog and tweet about their writing life. While that's interesting to other writers—and we do inhale a lot of books—you're not reaching out to your readers. Who—guess what—are not writers! And don't care about how your querying is going, or what your struggles with your plot and character development are. Don't get me wrong! If you like to write about those things, there's a place—amongst other writers.

As readers, what we do care about are other stories that consume our lives.

So go to Twitter and type in your favorite TV show, and check out how many other people are chatting about that show too! When you type in your show, add the hashtag # (also called the pound sign) before the word. So it would look like this: #Bones (for the TV show).

What are hashtags?

From Daily Writing Tips, I found a useful explanation of what hashtags are.

"Hashtags are simply a way of categorizing particular tweets by including within them a keyword prefixed with the hash or 'pound' (#) symbol. So, for example, tweets containing writing advice will often contain the '#writetip' tag. The point of this is to make it easier to find all tweets containing writing advice. Similarly, you could find a stream of publication tips by keeping an eye on tweets with '#pubtip' in them.

"Using relevant hashtags in your own tweets also increases the likelihood of others seeing your post and becoming a follower.

They're a great way to engage with a particular

community of Twitter users."

More here: WWW.DAILYWRITINGTIPS.COM/40-TWITTER-HASHTAGS-FOR-WRITERS/.

I put this to the test and typed in #Firefly. Remember The TV show? Browncoats unite! This show has been off the air for years, but has developed a cult following. (Yes!) And yes, people are still chatting about it on Twitter. I joined in! Another show I chatted about with fans was Dr. Who. I typed in #DrWho and #DoctorWho and found out the trailer for the new season has been released. Cool! (Sigh! Yes, I'm a huge fan of the current series.)

What's the point? You may be asking. Well, as Daily Writing Tips said, I connected with new folks who may become my followers on Twitter. And most importantly, I connected in a real way, with all my enthusiasm, with other like-minded people.

Social media, as any social media expert will tell you, is all about being social. Making connections. Ironically, we're spending more time apart, isolated, tapping away at our computers, tablets and phones. What we really want, what we've always wanted, and need more than ever is to be connected, to be a part of the human tribe.

As a result of my chatting about favorite Young Adult (YA) books, I learned of a new series to check out, The Queen's Thief, and gained some fans in the prospect, other people who love reading

YA as much as I do. And it just so happens that I write YA fantasy, too.

Here are some tips on how to make hashtag connecting fun and related to your ultimate goal of selling books. (That is your ultimate goal, right?!)

1. Choose shows, books, authors, movies that you love! (Easy, right?)

2. Make sure your choices are related to what you write. If you write steamy romance set in contemporary United States, chatting about your love of Star Trek probably has no real relevance to the kind of books you write.

3. As a followup from #2, stay away from controversial topics that don't serve your author career. In the United States, that would be religion, politics and sex. Unless, like I said, these topics and related shows are directly related to your themes in your books.

4. When you tweet, post as a reader, the raving fan that you are.

5. Above all else, have fun!

So writers, go forth and connect with your buddies, other readers who are fans of the types of shows and books and movies you like.

(Inspired by author and teacher, Kristen Lamb (AUTHORKRISTENLAMB.COM/) who was doing her own Tuesday series. This chapter is from a series of posts I called Twitter Tuesdays.)

Activity Guide

☐ On Twitter, search for your favorite TV show, movie, or book.

☐ Use the name or title with a hashtag and participate in the Twitter conversation.

☐ Or just lurk with a smile on your face. #DoctorWho anyone?

Chapter 10: All the Good News That's Fit to Tweet: What to Say on Twitter

Many authors just getting started in marketing their books think that Twitter is a confusing beast. Twitter actually provides us with a wonderful platform to show off our writing skills 140 characters at a time, and still share a nugget.

Yet, there really is a simple way to know what to write. If you just follow these 3 rules of social media posting, you'll be highly respected by your readers:

- Give praise/gratitude to another (Mentioning other people by their Twitter name will ensure that your message will come to their attention.)
- Share a piece of useful news: yours or another's
- Toot your horn, requesting a looksee, pointing to your success, etc.

Examples

For each category, here are examples of my own tweets:

Good News

- Good News—wonderful news—for client Julia Schopick, author of Honest Medicine:

Effective, Time-Tested, Inexpensive Treatments for Life-Threatening Diseases
- Highlighting a new indie author, Revital Shiri-Horowitz, author of Daughters of Iraq An enticing read opening our eyes to a little known community! amzn.to/iluz4e @GetGlue #DaughtersOfIraq

Share
- Submit your story to Stephanie Chandler's anthology about why you chose to leave a corporate job for self-employment
- Author and editor @KarysaFaire reveals why Writing Romance isn't for Wimps! haha! #amwriting #amediting #reading bit.ly/lwIS0c

Tooting My Horn
- Pimping my book's latest blog tour stop! Readers, comment to win a bk + enter the grand prize! #fantasy #YAfantasy Henrietta The Dragon Slayer by @Beth_Barany www.writersfunzone.com/blog/beth-barany-novelist/blog-tour/
- An Exercise from Twitter for Author: Social Media Book Marketing Strategies for Shy Writers bit.ly/TBUvV3 #amwriting #ammarketing

Activity Guide

☐ Compose three tweets: a "thanks" tweet; a "share a resource that's related to your mission" tweet; and, a "toot your horn and invite others to see what you've got" tweet.

☐ Then post them.

Chapter 11: More Examples of What to Say on Twitter

Many authors ask me what to write in their tweets. Hey, I get it, if you're used to writing 100,000 word novels, then writing a 140-character tweet can feel daunting and confusing. Where do you focus? How do you know what's important? And under these questions, I understand you may also be asking: What good is it for me to post on Twitter?

Here are some real tweets I generated. They illustrate the main principles to keep in mind. As mentioned before, they do one of three things: Give thanks; Share a resource that's related to your mission; Toot your horn and invite others to see what you've got. Something else they do is they express your value as expressed in your Clear Message, as I shared in Chapter 4.

Sample Tweets:
- A low-priced e-reader releasing on my birthday, June 17 bit.ly/bLpqlW
- Biggest users of $500 iPad? Kids reading books bit.ly/8YSHc3
- Remember Microsoft's Courier? Well, You Can Forget About It bit.ly/97Q5Rz
- Hrithik Roshan rocks! His latest film is coming to the SF Bay Area. The question is: will I drive an hour to see it ...

- Self-published authors to get in iBookstore via Smashwords bit.ly/bxnsdB
- If you love Bollywood, then you'll love Dhoom 2. If you've never seen a Bollywood film, I recommend starting with this bit.ly/blDsfE
- Face the scariest thing @ writing a bk now. #book writing #Writer's Adventure Guide tips bit.ly/a5x5eD
- How do you celebrate yr daily writing successes? #book writing #Writer's Adventure Guide tips bit.ly/a5x5eD

More tweets at
WWW.TWITTER.COM/BETH_BARANY.

Activity Guide

☐ Compose two to three tweets in Twitter.

☐ If you're ready, post them. Yep, hit that Tweet button.

Chapter 12: Don't Use Twitter If ...

If you don't want to have fun ...

If you don't want to connect with your colleague and other industry professionals.

If you don't want to experiment with writing in 140 characters or less. Less is better.

Don't use Twitter if you don't want to connect with your readers as a reader.

And above all, don't use Twitter if you don't want to connect with your current and potential fans about your gift to the world: your book.

Why else shouldn't you use Twitter?!

PS. This wasn't a chapter to brainwash you about how great Twitter is.

PPS. Whatever you do, don't read the rest of this book. It might inspire you to fall in love with Twitter, or at least make friends with it.

Activity Guide

☐ Whatever you do on Twitter, don't have fun. Just kidding.

Chapter 13: Dare to Play With Twitter: The Dirty Little Secret

Are you scared to jump into Twitter for fear of doing it wrong? Here's the Dirty Little Secret. We're all inventing how to use Twitter as we use it.

That's right ... we're playing, seeing what works. I know my tweets work when I receive a response from the people I'm looking to reach: my followers! And when people retweet my posts. And when people click on my links.

Question: How do you know what works for you on Twitter?

You get to define what success is for you in this realm, and in every realm of your book marketing strategy.

Another dirty little secret: We learn by copying our peers. At least I do.

I copy what I like and disregard the rest, after trying things out for myself!

Some of the people I've learned from, and continue to learn from:

- Tony Eldridge (TWITTER.COM/TONYELDRIDGE)—He has lots of tips about conducting Twitter contests. Check out his book, *Conducting Effective Twitter Contests: With Videos.*
- Patrick Schwerdtfeger (TWITTER.COM/SCHWERDTFEGER)—Author of *Marketing Shortcuts for the Self-Employed*

(2011, Wiley) and a regular keynote speaker for Bloomberg TV. His strategic advice is applicable to authors, because we're business people, after all. Right?

- Joel Friedlander (TWITTER.COM/JFBOOKMAN)— His post, 10 Tips For Getting Started On Twitter, is full of useful tips! (WWW.BOOKBUZZR.COM/BLOG/BOOK-MARKETING/10-TIPS-FOR-GETTING-STARTED-ON-TWITTER/)

Activity guide

☐ What are your thoughts on playing with Twitter as an author? Who have you learned from?

☐ Comment on Twitter using the hashtag #twitter4authors and I'll reply.

☐ You can also contact me directly on Twitter: TWITTER.COM/BETH_BARANY.

Chapter 14: Social Networking for Authors: An Overview on Author Branding

Now we're leaving the realm of Twitter only and entering the world of author branding.

A brand is a promise. For an author and speaker, your brand is a promise to your readers and listeners.

To discover and uncover your brand, I invite you to explore you, your author self, and your book through a series of questions that I present in the remaining chapters of this book.

For more questions to help you uncover your brand, be sure to check WWW.TWITTER-FOR-AUTHORS.COM.

Remember: There is no right answer to creating your brand. Only what is right for you. If you fake it, we will know.

This chapter is adapted from an article based on a presentation I gave to the Silicon Valley Romance Writers of America chapter on September 26, 2009 and is written by Nicci Carrera. I've adapted it for this book with her kind permission and am including it here because it's a perspective from someone new to social media book marketing—a useful perspective for other beginners to social media.

Beth Barany uses social networking for her business and now incorporates it in her work as a creativity coach. In her talk, she provided excellent insight into this exciting and important way to build an author platform.

At the start, Beth collected people's concerns, which consisted primarily of privacy and time wasting. "I'm a writer, I shouldn't be doing tweets." (Tweaks yes, tweets no.) Beth addressed these concerns and other minor ones as they arose.

Her first point was that social networking as an author means finding the right platform for you, not using everything that's out there. And her final point was, how do you know if online social networking is for you? If it's fun. If it isn't fun for you, don't do it! You can still use real-world networking and more traditional marketing such as postcards to announce your book.

What is Social Networking?

Beth discussed the meaning of social networking, for it is not confined to the Internet, of course. Examples of social networking included the very Silicon Valley RWA meeting in which we were participating as well as getting together with people for other professional meetings, such as writers' conferences. All of these activities are social networking. They all represent opportunities to share information and gain connections. Social networking facilitates information between users.

Online social networking is the same thing.

Before the Internet, people used things like postcards to get the word out about their new releases. Postcards are still a great thing to do even with the advent of the Net. The other great way books are sold, really the primary way books are sold, is by word of mouth. Think of using the Internet as word of mouse. (Editor's Note: This is a play on words on the familiar phrase "word of mouth.")

Now for some definitions. There's a difference between social networking and marketing. Social networking's purpose is to create connections, gather readers, and make friends. Marketing's purpose is to tell people to buy your book.

Marketing isn't about conversation, it's a one-way street.

Social networking is two-way communication.

Social networking involves a dialogue. People do business with people they know, like, and trust. An example of trust for authors is your consistent delivery on the promise of your brand. People will read your books because they know you are going to deliver on the goods, the emotional payoff. (Editor's Note: Our first and most important job as authors is to write the best book we can.)

Social networking provides an opportunity to expose yourself to a wider net (no pun intended). As you start your social media presence, you may notice that the number of people in your network tends to start off slowly and then grow exponentially. It's good to build yourself up—build your platform—before you are published. The more people you can demonstrate are paying attention to you, the better catch you are to a publisher and agent. Social media book marketing now is less advertisements and more conversation.

People have described social networking as tribes. Your tribe includes your readers. Also, build on your existing tribe, like the people in our RWA chapter, to start your social network foundation.

Social networking allows you to create a regular touch point with your fans and is an added component to our marketing as writers.

(Editor's Note: Perhaps most well known about this topic is Tribes: We Need You to Lead Us by Seth Godin.)

How to Use Social Networking

There are ways that you can make it easy and simple. Definitely get the book, *Webify Your Business* by Patrick Schwerdtfeger (expanded version released by Wiley as *Marketing Shortcuts for the Self-Employed: Leverage Resources, Establish Online Credibility and Crush Your Competition*).

Beth referred to this resource quite a bit for any technical questions. I have purchased it and started working with it and I highly recommend it as a hard-hitting, practical guide. By hard-hitting, I mean the author Patrick Schwerdtfeger, makes an unequivocal case for growing your business through the Internet. He makes it easy, breaking it down into sequential steps that include identifying your value proposition and synthesizing what you are offering into an elevator pitch.

Beth suggests that if you choose to use the Internet before you are published, it's good to choose a very broad brand, if you don't have a specific niche yet, so you don't limit yourself to a particular genre or type of book. "Aspiring Author" is a good one for starters.

To build your tribe, connect with other writers who write in your voice. Group blogs are great. If you write on a blog with authors who share a similar voice, readers of the blog will pick up your book, too.

When you start to use Twitter, her tip for not being bored by people's trivial posts, is to follow interesting people! On TWITTER.COM, you can follow book festivals, writers, editors, and other industry professionals. Follow an agent to see what your competitors are doing.

For privacy, on TWITTER.COM, you can block who follows you and you can use an alias.

The Uses of Twitter and Facebook

Beth uses Twitter to share what's going on in the industry. Twitter allows you to connect with your readers and Facebook helps you engage your community. (Editor's Note: This depends on your genre and can be the opposite.)

One writer created a whole Facebook page about her fictional world. This example raised the question of how to protect that world. You can't copyright an idea so be aware of that. Regarding protecting your copyright, you can register your book with the Library of Congress online at COPYRIGHT.GOV/. However, anything you create is copyrighted, by default.

Facebook can be used to share about your business, and what you are doing. *Webify Your Business* goes into this really well. This book offers an integrated approach to the Web. Patrick Schwerdtfeger has you plan what you are going to share on Facebook and on LinkedIn before you start.

Beth suggests talking to other authors who use Facebook and find out how they use it. For Facebook, the Profile page is more for personal stuff. You can create a Page for your business. The link to do so is in a box on the bottom of your Profile page. The Profile page should have some personal stuff. However, no one knew of anyone getting their Profile page canceled because it was strictly marketing. One author put the cover of her book on her Profile page.

If you have a blog, you can connect it to your Page. People can be a fan of your Page without being a friend.

Twitter is micro-blogging because it is limited to 140 characters. It has a real-time news feel to it. You can use it to share information. Use Twitter to create pass-along value. You can use it to communicate milestones. You can use it to talk about other authors.

Beth shines a light on other resources. In fact, being a resource is her brand. She aims to include a link in every tweet.

You can use LinkedIn.com to generate conversation. It's more of a community for professionals. If you use LinkedIn, use their groups. Gain visibility. Some groups are for writers and editors. You can find conversations there.

For blogging and online articles, you can write about writing. It's something you know something about! Then, when you're book comes out, you can say, "Oh by the way, I have a book coming out," to your network.

On Facebook, create a fan page.

Before you start to build your online presence, be sure to save a domain name with a web hosting company.

Time Strategies and Effectiveness Tips

For Twitter: Every day follow five more people that you like. Go to TWITTER.COM/BETH_BARANY and check it out. See who she is following.

There's an unwritten rule that about half the

people you follow will follow you. Set a timer and try to follow five people in five minutes and post one tweet. Do this daily, or if that's too much, do it once or twice a week. You can see what Beth has done. She creates tweets to be released later, at midnight and 6 a.m., which you can do by using WWW.SOCIALOOMPH.COM/ (or HOOTSUITE.COM/, Tweetdeck, or the like). If you're a working author, say something very interesting and specific about your book. Some authors use Tweets to create tension, for example saying, "I just had my hero get in a motorcycle accident, what do you think should happen next?" This draws people back and engages them in conversation. (Editor's Note: And your tweets reach a global audience.)

Another thing to tweet are resources, like Beth does.

For Facebook, go on it once a month or once a week and post something. Go to the homepage, it's everyone's feed. Set your timer for 15 minutes and friend around. Friend a few people. See what people are saying on the general homepage. Note that when you go to people's profiles or to the home feed, you can simply click a "like" button if you like what they have posted. Like Beth on Facebook (WWW.FACEBOOK.COM/BETHBOOKCOACH)!

For Beth, marketing takes up about a quarter of her time while a quarter to a third of her time is spent creating content.

Branding

Know where you stand. People want to know your flavor. Romance writers want readers to have fun. Ask yourself why you write. Again, Romance writers have an overall brand of feeling good.

When you are online, keep your conversation in your brand. Also, keep your tweets professional. (Editor's Note: A good resource on author branding is an article by Jenn Stark, "Brand Marketing Made Easy" WWW.OUTCOMEBRANDING.COM/BRAND-MARKETING-MADE-EASY/.)

Other Resources

There's a Muse Online Writers conference in the second week of October. It's probably filled up, but you might still be able to get in. It's online, it's free. There are publishers there, they take pitches, a lot goes on there. You can present also, by getting in touch with the organizer in advance. (Editor's Note: Connect with Muse Online Writers Conference here: THEMUSEONLINEWRITERSCONFERENCE.COM/.)

Beth is part of a newsletter called Heart of the Bay, put out by the San Francisco chapter of the Romance Writers of America. More information about that group here: SFARWA.NET/.

If you do an online search, there are lots of articles on social networking.

The Romance Writers of America

WWW.RWA.ORG/ has a Facebook page here: WWW.FACEBOOK.COM/ROMANCEWRITERS.

Check out TRIBALAUTHOR.COM/. (Editor's Note: An innovative way to connect authors and publishers.)

If you have questions, you can email Beth at beth@bethbarany.com.

Chapter 15: Play a Game You Can Win: Social Media Book Marketing Strategies for Shy Writers

Often approaching something new as a game can create a spirit of experimentation and help you get into action.

That's the spirit of this chapter and of much of my work with authors.

You're in charge of your schedule. You are, aren't you? (Minus the day job, if you have one, and the commitments you have to your family.) So set up a game you can win around social networking.

I'll give you the shortcut right here at the beginning: Just setting up a goal and taking action toward your goal is how you win!

For those of you who want the "how," I'll share how to set up your goals and give you some strategies and tips to get into action now so you can accomplish them and sell more books. The number one thing to focus on is to set a goal.

First, some guidelines about setting your goal.

Overall, I recommend you make your goal one hundred percent attainable and fun. While my goals look like tall mountain climbs to most people, they are manageable and attainable goals to me. For beginners, your goal could be to get familiar with the lay of the land of social networking. For advanced users, I recommend you challenge yourself to have even clearer goals and higher numbers to reach.

Playing a game you can win has four main steps:
1. Setting up the game
2. Playing the game
3. Tracking your wins (or losses)
4. Evaluating the game.

Note: Winning means doing the actions you decide to do. The bonus is the increase in followers and subscribers, and book sales.

1. **Set up the game.** Because this is your own game, this means setting up the rules, parameters, how to win, etc. Decide the parameters for these three factors:

*Time Commitment: Decide the start and finish date for your game, and how much time per session you'll play. Write down the action you will take and by when. The reason for this is that you want to create good habits for your long-term success. As social media book marketing becomes part of your marketing outreach in the way that works for you, these actions will become part of your toolkit within easy reach.

Recently, during a blog tour for a client that I ran as part of her national re-launch, we put our attention on increasing her Twitter followers, Facebook likes, and blog subscribers. Through our social media marketing book efforts, we increased her Facebook fans by over thirty percent, her Twitter followers by forty-six percent, and quadrupled her book sales.

For example, start on the first of the month and finish at the end of the month; and commit to 30 minutes a day four days a week. Another example: you can decide to spend 30 minutes a week on your social media book marketing strategies, once a week on Twitter, and the same amount of time on Facebook. You win by visiting at least five friends in each location and interacting with them, if only to click "like" on something they wrote on Facebook, or to just read their post on Twitter.

*Winning Actions: Be specific. Choose an action that someone outside of you could identify as an action.

For example, your actions could be: posting tweets, friending/following, posting on Facebook, blogging, etc.

*How to keep score—tracking: I recommend using a simple spreadsheet to track your time and your stats. A template "Tracking Social Media Stats" is available at online at www.TWITTER-FOR-AUTHORS.COM.

For a beginner with social media, winning for you may equal just putting in the time to get familiar with these platforms. And for those of you that find all this really scary, your game can just be: get clear on your fears and concerns, acknowledge them, and ask, "How are your current feelings doing a very good job of keeping you safe?" I am not at all mocking those feelings, but honoring them. Start from where you are. (That's the first lesson and stage of my book, *Writer's Adventure Guide: 12 Stages to Writing Your Book*.)

2. **Playing the game.** This is where you get into action! I highly recommend you make this action be the smallest step that you can take, that this step feels the safest you can choose, and that this step be one that allows you to still make progress toward your chosen goal. Many success teachers insist that those who write down their goals are more likely to achieve them.

3. **Tracking your wins (or losses).** Keep track in a spreadsheet, in your journal or agenda, or a postie. What matters is you choose a method that works for you. Celebrate your actions, no matter how small. According to trainer, author and musician, Robert Fritz, author of *Your Life As Art* and other books, the little successes count just as much if not more to the subconscious part of us that says Yes! to everything we feed it.

And yes, celebrate your wins! Tell your loved ones. Tell your new Facebook and Twitter buddies! We will cheer with you.

If social networking and online book marketing feels like drudgery to you, or if you're afraid of stepping your toe in that pond, then I recommend you find supportive peers, a coach, or a teacher to walk you through it. That way you can use this low cost simple way to get the word out about your books to the wide world.

4. **Evaluating the game.** On a regular basis evaluate how well your social media steps are doing based on the goals you set. You may want to evaluate monthly, or quarterly, and then make adjustments based on what's working well, and let go of what's not working for so well.

Above all, have fun!

Activity Guide

☐ Ask yourself: How can I make social media book marketing fun for myself, or make it even more fun?

☐ Take at least one action to put that fun into place.

Chapter 16: Discover Your Book Promotions Style by Copying, I Mean, Following the Masters

You may think that promoting your book is a pain-in-the-you-know-where, but you may be trying to force a round peg into a square hole. If you just focus on your strengths and communicate them through some of the best social media tools out there, you will be able to become more visible to your ideal readers, and ultimately, sell more books.

When my book first came out, *The Writer's Adventure Guide*, I so didn't want to promote it in ways I thought we authors we're supposed to. I didn't send out any review copies, had no guest blogger interviews lined up, and couldn't conceive of doing a book signing.

But then I realized that if I promoted my book using my strengths—teaching—I would feel comfortable. In fact, I tied my book release with my workshop at the national Romance Writers of America conference in Washington D.C. (As an independent author/publisher, I have the ability to release books on the date I want to.) Teaching and speaking have become one of my main ways of promoting my business and my books.

Now, I realize that teaching and speaking is not what every author wants to do.

The big question is: What are your strengths?

Writing as Your Promotions Strength

Yes, writing is one of your strengths. Hmmm.

With your skill of writing, my dear shy writers, how can you get the word out about your book? Peruse this list and see if there is one activity that you can do at least once a week. By the way, if you don't know where to begin, ask writers you know who are active in the below areas for tips. I learn a lot from observing my colleagues.

- Blogging, either for your blog or as a guest on others' blogs. I run an active blog for writers called the Writer's Fun Zone: WWW.WRITERSFUNZONE.COM/BLOG
- Facebook: Write snippets about your book, your writing process, or about your passions that relate to your book.

I recommend you follow the example of writers who have a big following, like Eloisa James, (her Facebook Fan page: WWW.FACEBOOK.COM /ELOISAJAMESFANS), Julia Quinn (Facebook Fan page: WWW.FACEBOOK.COM/AUTHORJULIAQUINN), and Anne Elizabeth (Facebook profile page: HTTP://WWW.FACEBOOK.COM/ANNE.ELIZABETH.9678).

- Twitter: Share research, hobbies, passions that relate to your book, but also to your personality. As Kristen Lamb points out in her book, We Are Not Alone, readers connect to us on personal levels, too.

Check out how these very prolific Twitter users

are using Twitter to interact with their fans and readers: (I chose them because they have fun engagement styles.)

- Paul Dorset—TWITTER.COM/JCX27
- Paulo Coehlo—TWITTER.COM/PAULOCOELHO
- S.M. Boyce—TWITTER.COM/THESMBOYCE
- Lorna Suzuki—TWITTER.COM/LORNASUZUKI

Some of my hobbies that I like to share about on Twitter include: travel to Paris; coffee; quotes from books I'm reading that inspire and help writers; sharing about my favorite science fiction and fantasy TV shows, books and movies. (Doctor Who anyone?!)

- Commenting on other people's blogs: Even before your book comes out, you can use your writing to great advantage. Blogger and public relations specialist, Julia Schopick, shares tips on how to use commenting as an effective marketing tool in her post, "What makes a blog comment great??" WWW.WEBBASEDPR.COM/2007/12/WHAT-MAKES-A-BL.HTML.

Additionally, PJ Van Hulle, business development and marketing expert, encourages blog commentators to be "kind, courteous, and provide value."

- Video: Namely, YOUTUBE.COM. Did you know that YOUTUBE.COM is one of the largest search engines out there? (Number 2 as of mid-

2012). You may not be blogging or tweeting or facebooking, but you may perk up at the mention of video. Some authors I know who are using YouTube.com to increase their visibility: Liz Adams, Patricia Simpson, Graciela Tiscareno-Sato. Resource: Animoto.com. My husband uses this tool to great effect for his book trailers and the ones he creates for clients. We have a coupon for a discount on TWITTER-FOR-AUTHORS.COM.

Next question: What are your passions and hobbies?

Passions and Hobbies

My husband Ezra Barany, best-selling author of *The Torah Codes*, loves asking people "What are your hobbies?" in social gatherings.

I recommend sharing about your hobbies with your readers and potential readers. You never know what attracts people. Sharing about hobbies has the added bonus of geeking out about our passion, usually a very easy thing to do, thus bridging the place of not knowing what to say to spilling over with enthusiasm in your posts and tweets. ("Geeking out" is to "be or become extremely excited or enthusiastic about a subject, typically one of specialist or minority interest," according to OXFORDDICTIONARIES.COM.)

It's fun, too, to get with like-minded hobbyists and let them know you're an author.

Activity

Assess your other strengths besides writing, and pick one activity you can do weekly.

For example, author Rachael Herron (the Cypress Hollow novels from HarperCollins): While she indeed loves Twitter, she is also an avid knitter. She visits knitter groups, bonds with the ladies there, and voila, brings new readers into her sphere.

(Twitter.com/RachaelHerron)

Who do you admire in the social media space for coming across the way you'd like to be?

Follow the Leader

When we were kids, my younger sister followed my brother and me around. She wanted to be like us. When we played dress-up, she had to play, too. When we played hide and seek, she cried if we didn't include her. My sister learned to be a big girl from being around us. No, she didn't learn bullying from me. Okay, a little.

We all learn by following those who know more than we do. Who can you follow in your genre that you admire? Copy them like when you were little. Don't be shy. That's how we humans learn.

It All Comes Down to Love

While you're copying, you may discover that you are organically growing your author platform while communicating what you love.

PS. A great resource for organically growing your platform is Christina Katz's book, *Get Known Before the Book Deal*. I've written a book review of her book here:

WWW.WRITERSFUNZONE.COM/BLOG/2010/05/11/GET-KNOWN-BEFORE-THE-BOOK-DEAL-A-BOOK-REVIEW/.

Activity Guide

☐ What do you love talking to your friends about? Take that onto Twitter.

Chapter 17: Unpublished Authors Can Promote Too!

What can an unpublished author do to promote when there's no book?

You may think that book promotions start when your first book is coming out. In fact, book promotions start as soon as you decide to be a published author. If you just institute a few simple systems, you will be prepared to tell the world about your first book, lay the foundation for success for your entire writing career, and get noticed as being a writer long before your first book contract (or when your first book is released, if you're an independent author).

Why should you start now instead of waiting until you sign your first contract? After authors have signed a contract with a publisher, first-time authors are often scrambling to get a website up, their mailing lists together, put up social media profiles and gain followers, and complete their contracted books, all in a short span of time. Whew! A stressful situation, to say the least. Maybe the author is even caught short financially while they meet all these obligations. Marketing your first book and establishing a name for yourself can be a heady and overwhelming experience, especially while finalizing your first book for publication.

Like a mighty oak, you can plant the acorn of your success now, long before you're published and let it grow steadily over time, allocating resources in a steady drip.

Why not do all you can to ensure your success and start building and growing your success today?!

Choose at least one action from the menu of options, and tailor it to you. This chapter mentions four options: build your list, write articles, have a blog or site, use social networking. My criterion for choosing what to do is based on what is fun for me to do. What is your criterion for choosing what to do? Do you choose what is fun, or what is about freedom? Or perhaps you choose what to do based on ease, or time. Spend a moment to think about your criterion for choosing.

Establish a Presence

You probably have an expertise besides writing fiction, so you can start being viewed as a writer now. This benefits you internally—you get to see your name in print—and externally: you get to develop a presence and a following, and even feel accountable to your new following. Even without a site, blog, or list, you can write articles for newsletters, your local paper, or blogs. You can start with your local writing chapter's newsletter, if they have one, if you belong to the Romance Writers of America (RWA), Mystery Writers of America (MWA), Science Fiction & Fantasy

Writers (SF&F), Society of Children Book Writers & Illustrators (SCBWI), etc.

Long before I started writing books helping writers, I wrote articles for writers in my local RWA chapter newsletter, Heart of the Bay, for the San Francisco area chapter (SFARWA.NET). If you'd like to write articles too, you can also write for other bloggers. For example, I accept guest bloggers on my blog, the Writer's Fun Zone (WWW.WRITERSFUNZONE.COM/BLOG). I know many other bloggers who do, too.

You can also submit articles to article databases like EzineArticles.com, and ArticlesBase.com. (More information here: HubPages.com/Hub/Top-10-Article-Directories.)

Your Online Home

Whether you like it or not, nowadays we all need an online presence to be viewed as credible. Create a site that is sticky, meaning you change your content often and invite people to return and see what's new. Wordpress is great for this. I've seen Weebly used as well. Wix.com is another option. Inviting people to connect, comment and share is important because this helps you develop a relationship with your readers. While unpublished in book form, what do you put on your site? The basics: a home page, a bio, an about your work page, tips for writers, and a contact page. A good example is Vanessa Kier, WWW.VANESSAKIER.COM.

Like Vanessa did, you can also repost your articles on your site.

Social Networking

Where does your prospective readership show up online? Go there and start interacting. Lots and lots of your prospective readers are on Facebook. For those of you who hate Facebook, sorry. As you may have already heard, Facebook is a raging river, as Patrick Schwerdtfeger says. Patrick is an internationally sought-after speaker and the author of *Webify Your Business*, now updated and re-released by Wiley as *Marketing Shortcuts for the Self-Employed: Leverage Resources, Establish Online Credibility and Crush Your Competition*.) You may also want to consider Twitter, Goodreads or LINKEDIN.COM, depending on the audience you'd like to reach. I recommend you pick an online site that you enjoy, and go there to chat with your friends, reach out to new ones, and share your writing journey, and favorite reads.

Build Your List and Use It

Author of *Lady of Devices: A steampunk adventure novel (Magnificent Devices)* and the *All About Us* series, Shelley Adina, asked me for my mailing address. That was seven years ago. Every time she has a new book coming out I get a pretty postcard in the mail. Many authors prefer to use an email list instead of a mailing list, and have a signup box on their site or blog.

MAILCHIMP.COM is an affordable and easy-to-use newsletter service to start with.

Be sure to set up an RSS feed on your blog, too. Also use your email system (Outlook, Gmail, etc.) to organize and make current all the contact information of the current fans you may not even know you have: your close friends, family, and community acquaintances. You could also use a spreadsheet to keep track of your fans. The important thing is to be collecting folks and adding them to your database. Be sure to ask at your local writers' chapter if you can add them to your reader database, like Shelley asked me years ago.

You can start your promotional efforts now. You may as well use one of the approaches described here and stick with it over time. After all, you probably wrote your book that way. Put down roots, grow your database and writer presence, and grow your mighty oak of fans with care and attention. Then you will be ready when you sign your first book contract, or as an independent author, when you release your first book, to tell all your fans about the good news.

Activity Guide

☐ Pick one activity to start building your online presence and practice it diligently for one to two weeks.

☐ If you don't like it, switch to something you think you'll like better and take action on that.

Chapter 18: How to Find Your Readers Online

In today's market, it's essential that the author understand how to engage their audience directly, no matter how they're published. Once you know who your audience is and how they want to be communicated to, you'll be able to connect with them in just the right ways so that your sales numbers will increase.

This chapter has lots of questions for you to get started.

So the question to ask is who is your readership? Be specific. Know such details as:

- Gender
- Age
- Where they live
- Education level
- Socio-economic status
- Jobs held
- Reason for reading your type of books, and reading in general
- What else they read (other books, magazines, sites, etc.)
- Beliefs about life, love, family, religion
- What they really want out of life
- Favorite vacation spots
- Hopes, desires and dreams
- Fears and concerns

To go about finding such information, ask people. If you're an as yet unpublished writer, ask your early readers. Young women in their late teens and early 20s respond with great interest when I share tidbits about a paranormal YA I'm working on. For the published authors, you can run surveys on your site using services like WWW.SURVEYMONKEY.COM, which has an easy-to-use free version, and you can ask your readers at book signings, and the like.

Other ways and places to find your readers and make some educated guesses about who your audience is:

- Lurk in bookstores and libraries, book sections of supermarkets, Target etc. Watch who picks up books like yours. Watch them. Use your people watching skills to fill out the details listed above.

- Go to book reviewer sites to find your readers and make some educated guesses about who your audience is. Here's a list of a few I've gathered, collected in a Twitter list: I did a search for "romance book review blogs" and came up with a huge list, of which four are listed here:
  SIRENBOOKREVIEWS.BLOGSPOT.COM;
  SMARTBITCHESTRASHYBOOKS.COM;
  LIKESBOOKS.COM;
  DEARAUTHOR.COM/WORDPRESS.

- Talk to your librarian
- Talk to your independent booksellers

Chapter 18

As to answering the question on how they want to be communicated to, what I mean is how do your readers want to stay informed about your upcoming releases, book signing, etc?

The best answer to this is to give them choices. Connecting with you via Facebook, Twitter, a newsletter, a blog, are all options that different readers may take. Notice which of these mediums has or gets the largest numbers, and use that as your primary funnel, with everything else acting as a support. Or, you can duplicate the same content across multiple channels, using tools like Hootsuite, Seesmic, or SocialOomph.com.

For example, Eloisa James (www.EloisaJames.com/Contact.php) encourages contact with her in a lot of different ways: a newsletter for book releases; a forum for avid fans; a Facebook Fan page, and Newsflashes, which is actually her RSS feed. I like that: Newsflashes! I enjoyed reading Eloisa's FB posts, especially the ones about her European summer, though everything she posts is fun! I notice that Eloisa offers different information via different channels. Her web design team probably has tested out a lot of different ways, or just made educated guesses, about what kind of readers want what kind of content. If you're like me, and you want nibbles, FB or her Newsflashes are good. If you absolutely need to know when her next book releases are, her newsletter is good. If you need to be talking about her books with others, probably her forum and her FB fan page are best for that.

Activity Guide

☐ Find 1-2 book blogger/book reviewer sites where your readers hang out.

☐ Make guesses about who they are based on comments and how the reviews are written.

☐ How do you like to stay connected to your favorite authors?

☐ How connected would you like to be to your fans, if time and money were no concern?

Chapter 19: Artist Entrepreneur: Build From Your Strengths, A Case Study

Many artists, authors included, go into art because they love it. But to build a business, sorry guys, love is not enough ...

What am I saying? It's passion that got me here in the first place, and I'm guessing got you where you are now. Passion and determination. And building on your strengths. That's such an abstract concept. Let's break it down.

It's a given that we're not all excellent at everything; what might work for me doesn't work for another. And yes, I'm talking about marketing, and blogging and social media for authors.

Case in point: A client came to me a few months ago knowing she needed to get more familiar and more comfortable using social media. She didn't get Twitter, and Facebook was just horrid with all those faces. And how was it different from Twitter anyway? And what's the deal about blogging? Did she have to reveal personal details about herself? What could she write about? And how did she get the American audience learning about her European books and other writer aliases?

She knew she needed to overcome her fear and confusion of social media and start taking some action steps because she was about to release over half a dozen books in her backlist. She'd written 25 books in her long writing career, and she had to get with the times. She was now a mostly independent author and couldn't rely on tools and support that didn't exist anymore, like publisher-sponsored book tours.

After I got clear on all her writing names and all her **titles** (wow!), together we came up with a strategy that focused on her strengths.

To get there I asked her questions like:

- What do you like to read? How do you find the books you read?
- What do you like to chit chat about with your friends and acquaintances? What could you spend all day talking about (when you're not writing?)
- What is unique about you that maybe you take for granted and is easy for you to talk about?

Together we found out that she likes to talk about her travels, certain time periods in history and her childhood in India. She also loves to talk about chocolate, the inspiration for her books, the settings for her stories, how to write romantic comedy, and how to write series.

I showed her how to write Tweets and Facebook posts that generate interest and conversation. She started blogging more. And the single most important thing we did for and with her was set up a summer/fall blog tour with book giveaways, to introduce her newly re-released series to an American audience. I also worked with her in our coaching sessions to become more comfortable with using social media. Twitter became fun, and Facebook became understandable.

As we rolled into the last few weeks of her blog tour, her newly re-released series got sales. Yippee! Additionally, for her new book just released, we'd been doing a Facebook and Twitter campaign and some blogging, and it was getting sales, too. Yeah!

More importantly, readers were discovering or rediscovering her and that made the author, Elizabeth Edmondson (also writing as Elizabeth Aston), very happy. (You can learn more about Elizabeth Edmondson and her books here: WWW.ELIZABETH-EDMONDSON.COM/EDMONDSON/.)

Activity Guide

☐ What are your strengths that maybe you take for granted? Things you do easily?

☐ Perhaps ask a friend or a colleague to help you identify them with you. Sometimes we need the eyes, minds and hearts of others to help us become aware of who we are. We are social creatures, after all!

Chapter 20: Indie Authors: What is Your #1 Tip for Marketing?

Since I'm always curious how others market their books, I asked my friends at the Indie Authors Unite what their #1 marketing tip was. Some of their tips relate to social media book marketing and are great examples of how authors are using the tools. Some tips are out in the real world. I've included them to remind you that book marketing happens in person, too. I highly recommend you develop and act upon a strategy for book marketing that includes a variety of online social media, print and in-person activities, that are right for you. (I've listed more resources at WWW.TWITTER-FOR-AUTHORS.COM.)

Here's what they had to say!

Faith Mortimer, author of the historical novel The Crossing, says to get out and address groups. She's given a short presentation to Ladies Luncheon Clubs and Book Clubs. She's off on a cruise and plans to address a group there and hand out business cards "to anyone reading with an e-reader at the four international airports" she'll be traveling through. She adds: "The writer MUST get out and about, marketing themselves and their book. It won't happen without some hard work!

For more information on Faith and her books

go to her site: WWW.FAITHMORTIMERAUTHOR.COM.

Suzanne Tyrpak, author of the historical suspense set in Rome, *Vestal Virgin*, GHOSTPLANESTORY.BLOGSPOT.COM/, says, "Becoming a member of the Kindleboards community has been the best promo practice for me. Not just posting about books, but getting to know people, picking up tips, learning and sharing information." (WWW.KINDLEBOARDS.COM/)

Mira Kolar-Brown, author of the mystery, *Lock Up Your Daughters*, writes:

"For those who do not write for mass market it's very important and extremely difficult to find a way to introduce themselves to their target readership, because those readers rarely trawl the Kindle Boards or even read e-books. For that reason I'm planning to have some printed books done in the near future too. In the meantime, I'm following the websites of those authors whose readership I'd like to share. I don't advertise there but I do hint in online discussion that I write books too and then just wait for someone to express an interest. It's a long and slow process, but I've made some sales on the back of it and had a good response."

Mira Kolar-Brown writes the Simon Grant Mysteries series, set in Northamptonshire, UK.

Al Boudreau, Author of the political thriller, *In Memory of Greed*, says:

"I find that Twitter is invaluable for promoting, but it must be done through conversations with fellow Twitter members, not sending endless tweets about your book. One must give before they expect to receive. I try to help promote other authors and produce blog posts that help others as well. It really seems to be working."

More about Al Boudreau and his books at: ALBOUDREAU.WORDPRESS.COM/.

David Lender, author of the financial thriller, *Trojan Horse*, says:

"The most important thing I've done is join the Kindle Writing Group on Facebook. It's given me an education and perspective on the ebook publishing and marketing process that would have taken me 10 times longer to get on my own. Second best thing I did was buy copies of 5 books I wanted to show up as "customers who bought this book also bought these books" on Amazon. Then I sent some money to 4 friends and had them do the same. That gave my book 5 thrillers as comparables from the start. One thing I hadn't expected from that was my book showed up on those books' lists as well, which got sales started with the right target segment readers. It cost a little money but I considered that a promotion expense."

Chapter 20

More on David Lender at his website: www.DavidLender.net.

Lia Fairchild, author of *In Search of Lucy*, states: "Learn everything you can from your fellow writers. Don't be afraid to ask them questions. They are usually very nice and helpful."

Sibel Hodge, author of the romantic comedy *Mr. Perfect Wedding*, says:

"For me I think it's been socializing with other readers and writers. Writing blog posts, interacting with others on forums and twitter about a wide range of topics (not constantly plugging your own books). First and foremost, though, you have to write a good book with a good blurb and good cover. Word of mouth is the most powerful form of advertising.

"Be yourself. Being comfortable in your own skin makes others comfortable with you, too. If people feel relaxed and happy in your company, they will be more inclined to help you achieve your goals. Always treat others ... as you expect to be treated yourself. Remember that no one is above or below you. The only time we should be above someone is when we're bending down to pick them up. Be honest and share yourself with others. If you are a genuine person who helps out others, you will be more likely to achieve personal success."

More on Sibel Hodge and her books at: WWW.SIBELHODGE.COM.

Thea Atkinson, author of *Formed of Clay: an ancient novella of betrayal* (book 1 in the Flesh of the Gods series) dittos Sibel. She says, "I started selling when I began networking and helping others out. The old pay it forward AND pay it back approach."

More on Thea Atkinson and her books at: THEAATKINSON.WORDPRESS.COM/.

Mark Adair, author of the thriller *The Father's Child* says, "Being transparent might be number one for me ... inviting them into your journey and helping them with theirs."

For more on Mark Adair and his books, go to: MARKADAIR.COM/.

L.C. Evans, author of the Leigh McRae horse mystery *The Witness Wore Blood Bay* adds, "Don't try to go it alone."

Debbie Bennett, author of the psychological thriller *Hamelin's Child*, says:

"My number one tip—Be brave! It's like admitting I'm a closet alcoholic at work, finally admitting to my secret other life of being a writer. It's about being proud of the fact and not worried about what people might think about *me* when they read my story. Especially given the controversial nature of what I write."

More at: WWW.DEBBIEBENNETT.CO.UK/.

Seb Kirby, author of the thriller *Take No More*, says "Top tip: work hard. Join a network of like-minded authors like Indie Authors Unite."

Activity Guide

☐ If you have a book marketing tip of your own, share it on Twitter using the hashtag #twitter4authors.

☐ You can also share with me directly at beth@bethbarany.com, or on TWITTER-FOR-AUTHORS.COM.

Hurrah

Thanks for reading this book! I hope you found value and many useful activities to invite you to action.

Activity Guide

☐ If you found value in this book, please post a review. Thanks!

☐ You can find extra resources for *Twitter for Authors* here: WWW.TWITTER-FOR-AUTHORS.COM.

Credits

Earlier and shorter versions of some chapters first appeared in the Creativity Coaching Association newsletter and the Writer's Fun Zone blog: WWW.WRITERSFUNZONE.COM/BLOG.

"Using Twitter to Network and Market Your Books" first appeared in Heart of the Bay, the newsletter for the San Francisco chapter (WWW.SFARWA.NET/) of the Romance Writers of America WWW.RWA.ORG/.

"Social Networking for Authors: An Overview;" Adapted from an article based on a presentation I gave to the Silicon Valley Romance Writers of America chapter (WWW.SVRWA.COM/) on September 26, 2009. Written by Nicci Carrera.

Acknowledgements

Thanks to my business trainers over the years who introduced me to the world of the entrepreneur: Jeff Slayer and Kane Minkus at WWW.JEFFANDKANE.COM; Bryan Franklin, WWW.BRYANFRANKLIN.COM; Cheryl Liquori, my partner in crime at WWW.BREAKFASTBLOGGING.COM; and Patrick Schwerdtfeger, friend, author, and great teacher: BOOKPATRICK.COM.

Thank you to Ezra Barany, my husband, fellow author, cover designer, and cheerleader extraordinaire, and personal editor, without whom my life as an author entrepreneur wouldn't have been possible.

Thank you to my beta readers: Andrea Stenberg, Carissa Weintraub, Cathy Stucker, Cheryl Derricotte, Dan O'Brien, Doug Skinner, Ezra Barany, Ginny Gielow, Kymberlie Calkins Ingalls, Jennifer Carlevatti Aderhold, Julia Schopick, Lisa Young, Prudence MacLeod, Susan Swift, Toni Camilleri. And thanks to Anastasia Pergakis or ANASTASIACREATIVES.COM for her invaluable layout help.

About The Author

Certified Master NLP Practitioner and Creativity Coach, Beth Barany is the bestselling author of *The Writer's Adventure Guide: 12 Stages to Writing Your Book*, and *Overcome Writer's Block: 10 Writing Sparks To Ignite Your Creativity*.

Beth speaks to groups and conferences all over the San Francisco Bay Area and across the United States and Europe. Beth Barany is also an award-winning novelist. Her young adult epic fantasy novel, *Henrietta The Dragon Slayer*, won the 2012 Grand Prize in the California Book Fiction Challenge.

To connect with Beth on Twitter and ask her questions, contact her at:
TWITTER.COM/BETH_BARANY.

More about Beth and how she helps authors create successful careers at WWW.BETHBARANY.COM.

For goodies and resources about Twitter mentioned in this book, go to WWW.TWITTER-FOR-AUTHORS.COM.

beth@bethbarany.com
WWW.BETHBARANY.COM
TWITTER.COM/BETH_BARANY
WWW.FACEBOOK.COM/BETHBOOKCOACH

Excerpt of

Overcome Writer's Block: 10 Writing Sparks To Ignite Your Creativity

Introduction

Purpose of this writing guide

Welcome! You have come to the right place to overcome your writer's block and spark your creativity in unique ways.

This writing guide is written for writers, though all the suggestions can apply equally to other artists. Replace writing with your art, and go for it!

Views on creativity

I believe we are all creative. Yes, even you, in your time of feeling most blocked. Creativity is our birthright! We are here to play and be 100% ourselves. In this I act as your guide, mentor, coach, buddy, and teacher. My purpose is to help you to reawaken your playful self in your every day writing sessions. Let me help you to bring play into your work. With courage and kindness, with joy and spirit, I guide you on the writer's adventure. My specialty is storytelling via writing. My passion is book writing. A Certified Creativity Coach, writing teacher, nonfiction and fiction writer, and speaker, I am a communicator who writes and speaks to entertain, motivate and move others. I invite you to come play with me.

This writing guide offers a unique approach to writer's block. Since I believe we are all creative, and writers have the unique tool of writing it all out, the way through writers block is a multi-pronged approach, with writing exercises, finding your passion exercises, and some good old-fashioned goal-setting thrown in there for good measure.

How to Use This Writing Guide

Read this writing guide from cover to cover, or jump randomly from spark to spark. It's meant to support you, ignite your passion for writing, and help you write again. As you are a creative being, the way out of writer's block involves using your creativity in fun, unique ways.

Most of my suggestions and writing exercises can be applied in short 15-20 minute chunks of time while you're on a lunch break, sitting in the dentist's waiting room, or have a few minutes before the work day. Experiment with implementing the sparks once a week to enliven your writing sessions and keep things fresh. Refer to the sparks when you are having trouble getting started on your writing project.

However you choose TO use this writing guide, know that you are a creative being here to express yourself.

Express yourself. There is only one you!

Spark One: Organic Writing: The Garden Within

To grow the unique writer within, we need to look inward, and then take steps to cultivate our writer self.

As physical beings that are made up of atoms, molecules, elements and water, we are organic bodies of the earth. This we can't deny. Our creativity has roots in the earth and has grown organically from who we are and where we're from. Who we are as writers has grown from our lived experiences, our passions, our frictions, and your soil. How we've fertilized, what mental and emotional weeds we've pulled, how we've cultivated the gardens of our minds and hearts all contribute to who we are as writers. Who we are is the result of our fertilizer, our weed pulling, and how we tend our garden.

Your writing won't be like anyone else's, nor will your career, nor will your daily routine. This may appear self-evident, but don't we all compare ourselves to others, especially the best-selling writers? We often want to be like them: successful, writing guide in the front of the store, and great storytellers. So we think we need to emulate these bestsellers, and their routine, stories, and style. But we are not them; we didn't come from the same root stock, soil or climatic conditions.

Use the following questions and tips as guides to look inward and take steps to cultivate our writer selves.

Background

Consider where you come from. What is your background, family, education, your dreams, your cultural influences, that thing that happened to you, that thing you overheard, those family expectations, the whispers of your imagination? Be specific, be general, be wacky, be curious about yourself. Spill out the contents of your mind, and breathe. Stare off into space. Then look to see what you've written, and smile, or frown. These are your inspirations, your fertilizer, your individual quirks and quarks, interests, curiosities, knick knacks of the mind and heart. Your individual pattern, rhythm. Where you come from.

Motivation

Examine your deepest motivations for writing. What kind of writing do you want to do and do now, and why—what is your true motivation? Know why you write and don't take the first answer you come up with as the only answer. Dig deeper, listen harder, be truthful with yourself. The more you know your true motivation, the better your writing life, in that you can make excuses, but you can't lie to yourself anymore.

Discovery

Knowledge is powerful. What is your voice, your style, and what are your strengths, your weaknesses as a writer? As above, be as truthful as you can with yourself. No one will know these things but you. You are on a voyage of discovery and affirmation. Accept who you are. You are beautiful.

Three Tips to Cultivating Your Writing

Tip #1: Patience. The garden does grow itself. We don't stand by it every minute of every day and say, "Go roses! Go lavender! Grow!" It happens because of the proper conditions—the soil, the sun, the rain, and the seed. We shape the garden by our hand. We watch out for the dangers or bugs, and over- feeding or under-feeding. We care. We nurture. Regularly. As with gardening, so with writing. Show up for yourself. Honestly, why do you write? Could you not write? Probably not. In that case, make peace with yourself, and write. But be gentle. Plants do not grow faster if you pull on them. That would kill them. The most you can do is write regularly, with compassion, with awareness (tracking), and don't give up.

Tip #2: Compassion. Above all, be gentle, have compassion for the writer within, the writer you are growing, especially if you are starting out.

And especially if you've been at this for years. We tend our gardens day in and day out with care, giving the plants what they need, even if that rose bush has been there for years, or if you just planted it. Treat yourself no differently, especially if you're having a bad day, week, or month.

Tip #3: Trouble-shooting. Are there unhelpful pesticides—other people's ways, thoughts, ideas, beliefs that are not your own, or fatigue, overwork, not enough play—invading your garden? What hobbies can you give up to give yourself time to write? You can change many things that affect adversely your writer within—learn to say "No." The sun and rain, other people, world events, are factors beyond on our control. Accept that. If the soil needs amending, find the missing ingredients. Do you need to aerate—get out and do something new, something to expand your heart, mind or soul? Do you need to move your body to counteract an overactive mind?

Happy Cultivating the Writer Within!

More on *Overcome Writer's Block: 10 Writing Sparks To Ignite Your Creativity* go to www.BethBarany.com.

Get the Free Report:
"12 Stages of the Writer's Adventure™"

www.writersadventureguide.com

You can buy the book online at Amazon.com.

How to Run a
SUCCESSFUL
Blog Tour
For Authors

How to Run a Successful Blog Tour
for Authors

How to Run a Successful Blog Tour for Authors

In this 30+ lesson course, you'll learn how to run a successful blog
so that you can market your book to your readers.

bit.ly/SpecialBlogTourCourse $148

Original Price   Discount   You Save
$297   ↓ 50% $149

🔍 Free Preview   ♥ Wishlist   🎁 Gift

Spread the message about your book, generate book sales, and increase your fanbase!

Learn how to run a successful blog tour and promote your book!

This course is for:

- authors, fiction and nonfiction
- book marketers
- entrepreneurs

Not for absolute beginners, I'm assuming you have some comfort level with blogging, writing articles, and using social media, or you are ready to dive in and get comfortable with these tools fast!

3 hours of content!

I created 29 videos for you, anywhere from 1 to 11 minutes in length, so you can watch in short bursts, or watch the course all at once. It's about 3 hours of content. Block off your afternoon!

I also give you **Checklists** and **Templates**, and take the guess work out of what to say, to whom, and when.

Bonus: For those of you who sign up for my course, you get an e-edition of my new book, *Twitter for Authors: Social Media Book Marketing Strategies for Shy Writers*.

Just FYI... Normally I charge $997 to $2,500 to run these for clients, and in this course I've shared ALL my secrets. And if there's something you'd like to know about running blog tours, once you've enrolled you can ask live in the monthly calls or in the 24-7 forum that I check 3 times a week.

Go to http://bit.ly/SpecialBlogTourCourse to see if this course is right for you! (link is case sensitive)

30 Day Money Back Guarantee Lifetime Access - No Limits

Made in the USA
Las Vegas, NV
08 December 2021

36589631R00069